COPYRIGHT © 2022

MW00897453

PENGUIN

ペンギン

Pengin

SHARK

鮫
Same

MONKEY

猿

Saru

FOX

狐

Kitsune

RABBIT

ウサギ

Usagi

ELEPHANT

象

Zō

SQUIRREL

リス

Risu

MOUSE

ねずみ

Nezumi

SCORPION

狐

Kitsune

BUTTERFLIES

蝶

Chō

OWL

フクロウ

Fukurō

LIONESS

雌ライオン

Mesu raion

COCK

おんどり

Ondori

RHINOCEROS

サイ
Sai

WILD TURKEY

野生の七面鳥

Yasei no shichimenchō

SEAHORSES

タツノオトシゴ

Tatsunōtoshigo

SEAL

密閉する

Mippei suru

LADYBUG

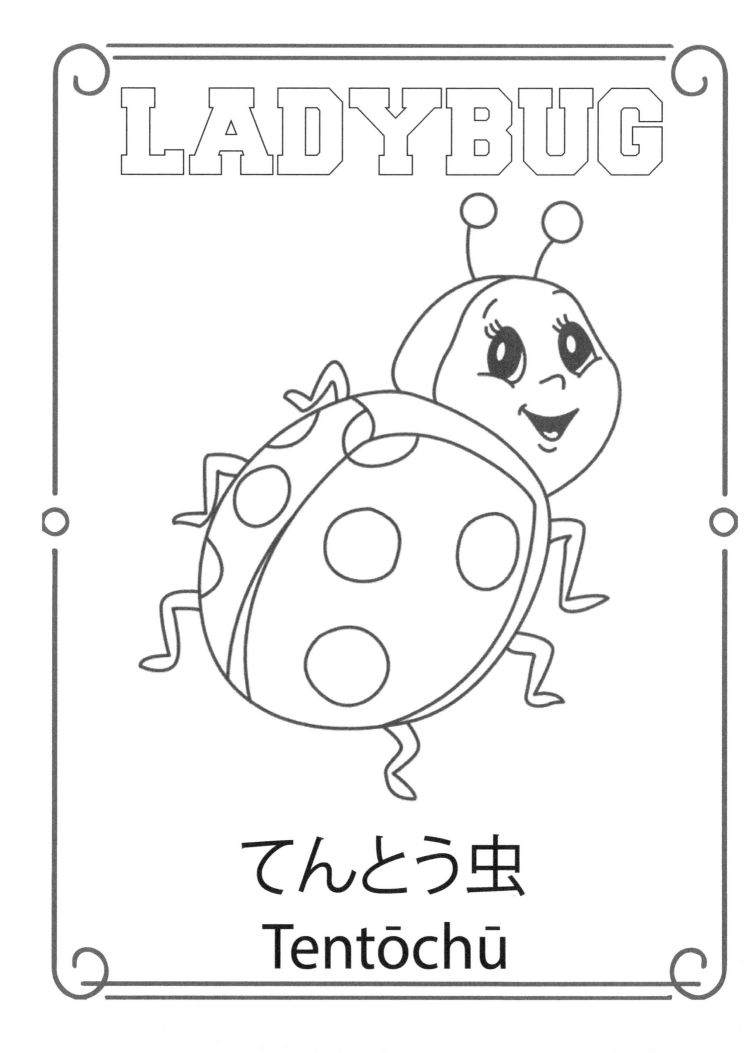

てんとう虫

Tentōchū

LIZARD

トカゲ

Tokage

TOUCAN

オオハシ

Ōhashi

BUFFALO

バッファロー

Baffarō

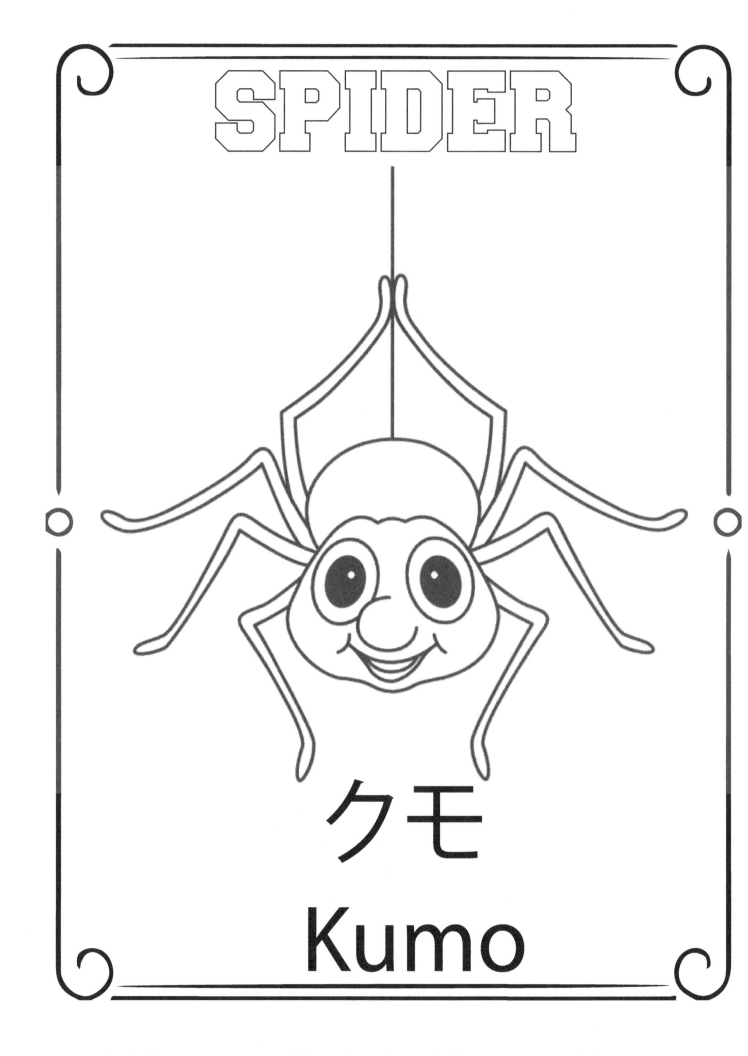

SPIDER

クモ

Kumo

ESCARGOT

エスカルゴ

Esukarugo

SHEEP

羊

Hitsuji

OCTOPUS

たこ
Tako

OSTRISH

ダチョウ

Dachō

OTTER

カワウソ

Kawauso

MEERKAT

雌ライオン

Mesu raion

MOSQUITO

蚊

Ka

LLAMA

ラマ

Rama

TURTLE

カメ

Kame

WARTHOG

イボイノシシ

Iboinoshishi

WALRUS

セイウチ

Seiuchi

MANATEE

マナティー

Manatī

PARROT

オウム

Ōmu

LEMEUR

キツネザル

Kitsunezaru

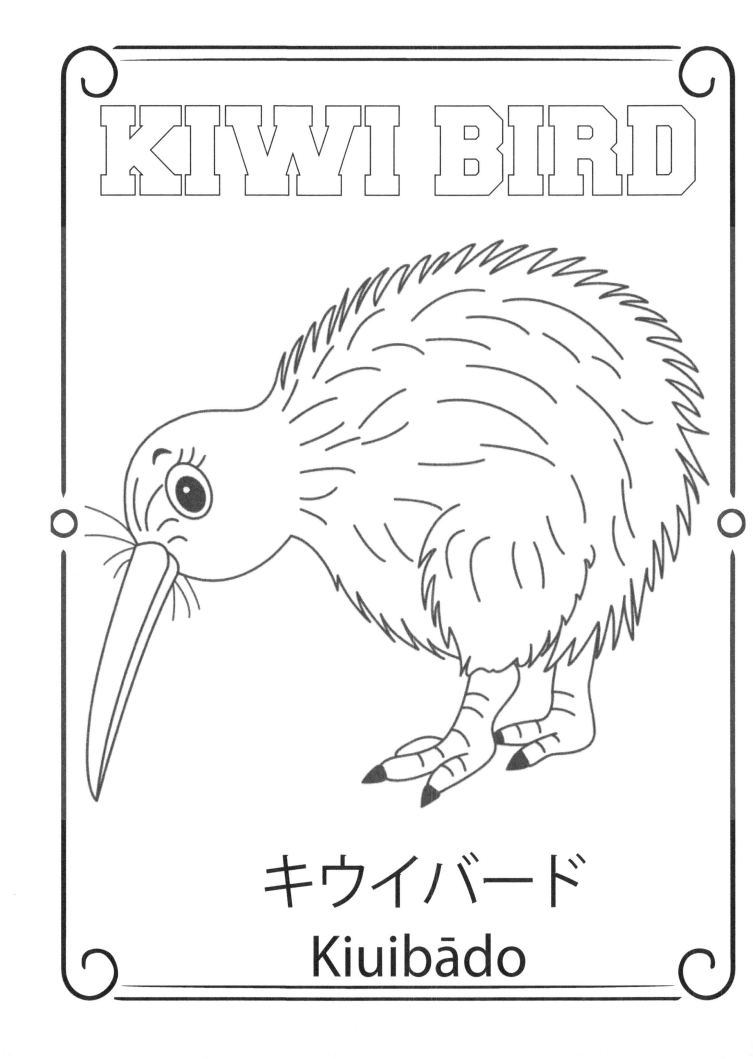

KIWI BIRD

キウイバード

Kiuibādo

Made in the USA
Las Vegas, NV
12 May 2024

89863034R00057